Those in this world who have the courage to try and solve in their lives new problems of life, are the ones who raise society to greatness. Those who merely live according to rule do not advance society, they only carry it along.

— *M.K. Gandhi*

Collins COBUILD

English Dictionary *for* Advanced Learners

spam /spæm/ **(spams, spamming, spammed)**
1 **Spam** is a cooked meat product made from pork and ham. [TRADEMARK]
2 In computing, to **spam** people or organizations means to send unwanted e-mails to a large number of them, usually as advertising. ❑ *...programs that let you spam the newspapers.* ♦ **Spam** is also a noun. ❑ *...a small group of people fighting the spam plague.*

fortunate /fɔːʳtʃʊnɪt/ If you say that someone or something is **fortunate**, you mean that they are lucky. ❑ *He was extremely fortunate to survive... Central London is fortunate in having so many large parks and open spaces... It was fortunate that the water was shallow... She is in the fortunate position of having plenty of choice.*

leading article **(leading articles)**
1 A **leading article** in a newspaper is a piece of writing which gives the editor's opinion on an important news item. [BRIT]
☑ in AM, use **editorial**

mere /mɪəʳ/ **(merest)**
Mere does not have a comparative form. The superlative form **merest** is used to emphasize how small something is, rather than in comparisons.

Over 110,000 references
- includes unique coverage of all word forms
- thousands of new words and meanings
- explanations in simple, natural English

Over 105,000 examples
- taken from the Bank of English
- helping learners with real English
- showing how each word is used

Comprehensive American coverage
- fully updated
- British and American usage clearly shown

2,800 usage notes
- giving information and guidance on real English

plus
- over 16,000 synonyms and antonyms
- essential grammatical information shown in unique COBUILD Grammar column
- additional help with register, frequency and usage
- clear layout for longer entries

Helping learners with real English

The Bank of English is a unique computer database which monitors and records the way in which the English language is actually used in the modern world. It is continually expanding and contains over 400 million occurrences of words, from contemporary British, American, and international sources: newspapers, magazines, books, TV, radio, and real life conversations - the language as it is written and spoken today.

Express Publishing

ISBN 0-00-761837-9

9 780007 618378 >

Collins COBUILD English Dictionary *for* Advanced Learners

Express Publish

RAJESH PILOT

In Spirit Forever ...

Sarika and Sachin Pilot
Remember ...

Lustre Press
Roli Books

ISBN: 81-7436-143-X

Lustre Press Pvt. Ltd.
M-75 Greater Kailash II (Market)
New Delhi 110 048, India
Phones: (011) 6442271, 6462782, 6460886
Fax: (011) 6467185, E-mail: roli@vsnl.com
Website: rolibooks.com

Produced at Roli CAD Centre

Printed and bound by Thomson Press (India) Ltd.

Jab tak kisanon ke bachche padh-likhkar un gaddiyon par nahin baith jayenge jahan se faisle hote hain, neetiyan banayi jaati hain, tab tak yeh desh upar nahin uth sakta.

(As long as children from villages do not occupy seats from where policies are drafted, no village will be able to show any gain.)

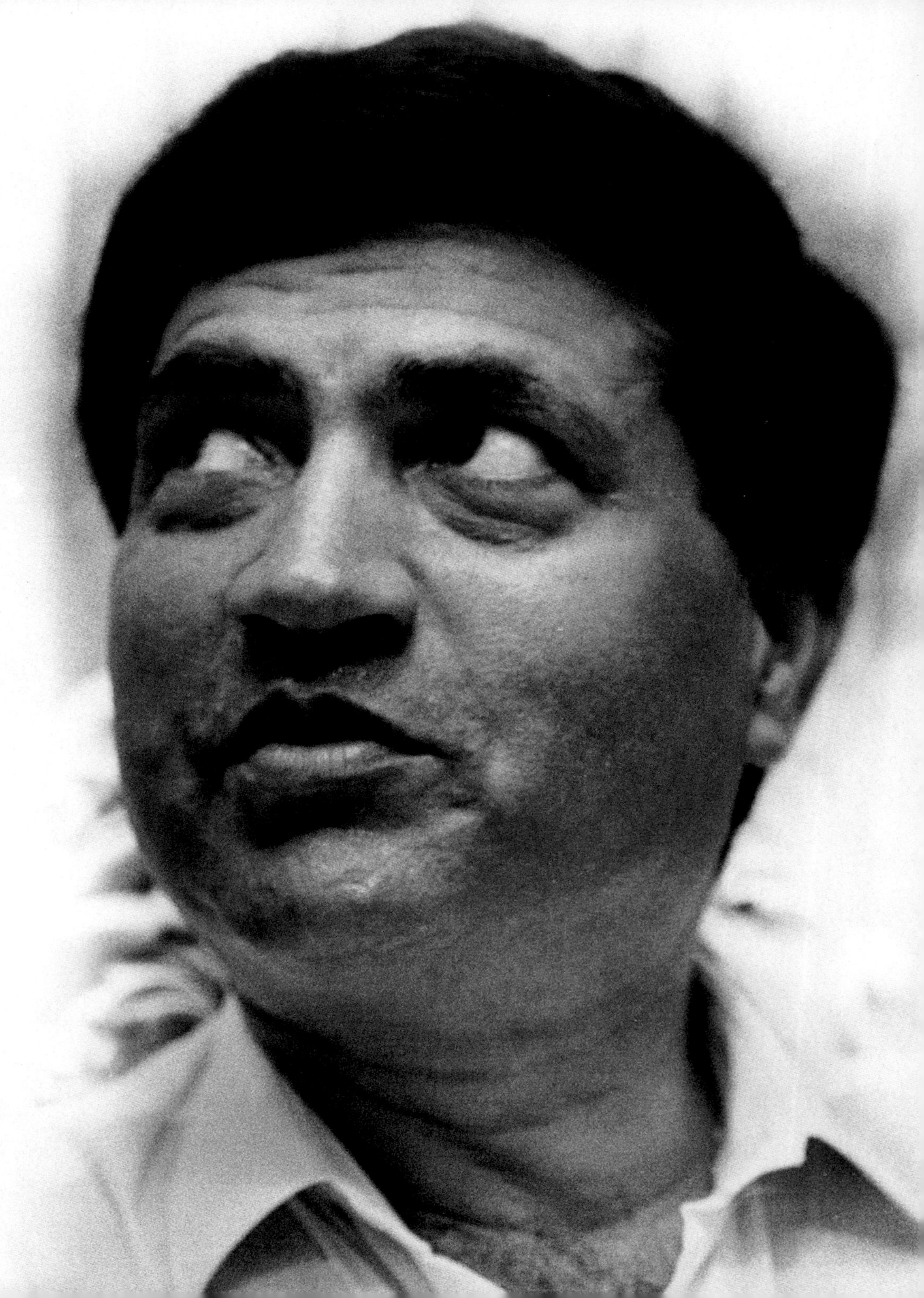

Growing up with Dad

Dad,

I never thought that, one day, I would write this.

As a kid, growing up, you don't think of your Dad as someone you will write about some day. At that time, Dad is someone you go to for everything; someone whose office you want to go and see, someone to play football with, someone who kisses you good night, every night. Most of all, he's someone you go to when Mom scolds you.

At least, that's what my father was to me. I still remember, every time he went out of town, Dad would bring back chocolates and comic books. He was my perfect Dad—as every father is for every child.

As children mature, they begin to *observe* their parents much more. At first, it was cool if Dad just let us do all the things that were important to us then: being allowed to stay up late watching TV, having a coke with our meals, getting a pet, owning a rugged terrain bike… But as time passed, I began to see the way my father functioned, took care of his family, handled his work. He was completely transparent in his attitude towards what he had chosen to do in his life, and in his interaction with his friends and relatives.

It was at that time that we began to learn from Dad—not merely things that he taught us consciously, but also those that we learnt merely as spectators, by just being there and observing his dealings in various areas of life. That was the point when we began to imbibe and emulate his forgiving nature, how to stand up to challenges—and to accept defeat and handle success in the same way that he did—by taking them in our stride.

We were fortunate that we were offered this opportunity from a young age, simply because Dad included us in his social life, and because he took out time to spend with us. There was a phase in our lives when we felt tied down by the extent of his affection and the time he spent with us. That was the time when we would have preferred to hang out with our friends and party. But whenever we did go out, Dad would insist that we come back home for dinner—no matter how late! Mom would come to our aid, saying we had our own lives to lead, but Dad would be obstinate enough to use—what we then considered—emotional blackmail.

Amazingly, we actually started to opt for staying at home as we began to enjoy our dinner conversations and debates. Subsequently, our friends too began to opt for coming to our home to enjoy the stimulus of our tête-a-têtes. What was wonderful was that it wasn't something we were forced to do, but *chose* to do. We spent some of the most memorable evenings of our lives by simply being at home. The transition from being Dad's children to Dad's friends was so natural, we never felt it happen. It was just there one day.

In hindsight, it is so obvious when and how it happened. It happened the day when we accepted his values and chose them for ourselves. It happened the next day when we saw him come to the support of a person who had always opposed his stance, and learned about forgiving our fellow beings. It happened, again, the day after that when we actually listened to his speech in a public meeting and realised that he repeated himself not because of his lack of convictions, but *because* of his own belief in those deep-seated convictions. And it happened once more when he reaffirmed that everything he had was because of God's grace, and that God is not someone you find only in a place of worship, but behind every move, every step that you take. And it has been happening ever since, even after Dad is no longer with us—just listening to people he worked with, helped, or had any relationship with is inspiring.

All fathers are great. So was ours. He taught us to respect life and the opportunities it offered us; he taught us to value fellow human beings; he showed us how to assemble a barbecue, to swim, to play *pithoo;* and he taught us about humanity. He showed us that no amount of work or help is ever sufficient, but that the satisfaction gained from it can prove enormous. He also taught us that it is the intention behind an action that defines the result. More important, he taught us to love—not just those people you are related to, or friends, but every one.

With our father, we learnt that at some level, all human beings are one, and that we are not really different from each other. With this learning came the intent to help others which, I now realise, was Dad's aim. We learnt that in our own way, we too could help people—if in no other way than in just hearing them out and lending them some moral support. I think my father's main aim was to help people and make them see how they could then help other people. And he taught this by example. For us, it was the most effective form of education. We can only hope that all those people whose lives he touched, can reach out to others in the same way. That, in real terms, would be Dad's most treasured dream realised.

Now that he is no more, every evening that we stayed home to have dinner with him feels even more precious. We were used to seeing Dad's pictures every day—in magazines and newspapers, official photographs, pictures that people had taken of him—but never imagined that one day we would be hunting for them to compile this book. A book that is a capsule of his life, his public service, and is dedicated to his enduring memory.

For us it has been a labour of love. We hope you too will enjoy these photographs.

Sarika

(Sarika)

Life with Dad

I could say thousands of things about my father, but writing them down like this seems the most difficult task in the world. For, in his passing, I feel a part of me has died too. In him, I have also lost my best friend. He was a successful politician, an inspiring leader, a pillar of strength and a generous soul—all locked into one. But for us, he was simply the best father anyone could have. No matter what his preoccupations, he was always there for us.

My father was one of twelve children—nine brothers and three sisters—that my grandparents had. Born in a village on the outskirts of Delhi, he lost his father at the age of eleven. From then on, tragedy was a constant companion for the family. Shortly after, my father lost all but one of his brothers. Therefore, at a very young age he was forced to shoulder the responsibility as the man of the house, even arranging for the marriages of his sisters.

Eventually, he left the village to come to Delhi to help his cousin with a small dairy in the vicinity of Birla Mandir. This was to prove the most difficult phase of his life. He worked ever harder to cope with the substantially higher standards of education in Delhi's schools while, simultaneously, working at the dairy and delivering milk twice a day to nearby areas.

His big break came when he applied for the armed forces and was selected. He qualified for both the army and the air force. My grandfather, himself a *havaldar* in the Indian army, would have liked my father to continue the tradition of joining the army but the substantially higher remuneration for pilots made my father make up his mind to opt for the Indian Air Force instead.

After his commission in the 96th course of the Indian Air Force, in 1966, my father became Pilot Officer Rajeshwar Prasad—a proud moment, indeed, not only for the family but the entire village.

He spent 14 happy years in the air force and saw action in the 1971 Indo-Pak war, something that I am really proud of. He was posted to various stations in the country, including Hyderabad, Delhi, Saharanpur, Guwahati and Kalaikunda. These were perhaps the most fun-filled years of his life. The friends he made in that duration remained his closest associates, lasting through his six terms as a member of parliament and ten years as a Central minister.

After quitting his job with the air force, he directed his energies towards politics. When he quit the air force, he had a wife, two children aged five and three, no pension, and certainly no political godfather. At that time most people thought him merely ambitious, and foresaw only uncertainty and frustration, but he braved their cynicism and 'sound advice' to make his foray into the world of politics.

People judge political success in terms of the power a person wields, but for my father, in the twenty years, five months and eight days of his political life, it is best measured in his ability to touch the hearts of millions of people and earn their good wishes. In that lay the key to his success.

He was dedicated to his job but I did not grow up with the feeling that he did not have time for his wife and children. We have been a very, very close-knit family and spent time together—be it travelling to Rajasthan by car or going underwater snorkelling in the Andaman Islands. For him, his family always came first.

We always had an open relationship with our father, being his worst critics as well as, hopefully, his most trusted advisers. But it was a two-sided relationship where he knew exactly what was going on in our lives. No wonder he was always there to share our joys and guide us through our rough patches. Our relationship was based on talking, confiding and sharing everything with each other.

He spent a lot of his time outside Delhi because he believed in reaching out to the people and making himself available to the masses. He would travel the length and breadth of the country, but would try and make it back home for dinner so that the family could have at least one meal a day together. On our part, we would often delay eating dinner even till past midnight just so that we could share the meal with him.

In his sixth year as Member of Parliament, he became Minister for Surface Transport. He went on to head the ministries of communications, internal security and environment. He was an able and effective administrator. During his tenures as minister, he brought with him new ideas and new initiatives that would revolutionise the future of the country forever. He was instrumental in taking far-reaching decisions, allowing the entry of cell phones, internet and wireless communication into the country. But his real interest lay elsewhere—amidst the poorer, underprivileged members of society whose lot he worked to improve. All through his political career, he championed the cause of farmers and labourers. Coming from a family that had lived through similar misery, he was able to empathise with their agony, and the poor from the remotest parts of the country, in turn, were able to associate themselves with him.

Having seen the love and affection that people had for him, it makes me proud to be part of his family. He gained his confidence not from political patronage but from the trust that people had in him. His inspiration came not from seats of power but from the drive to do something for his country. He had his reward not in the form of praise or admiration but from the heartfelt good wishes that people sent him. His satisfaction came not from electoral triumphs but from the blessings he received from the people.

He was a true nationalist and a staunch secularist. He was true to himself and to his principles and upheld them even while wading through the murky waters of politics. He had his convictions and fought hard to stick to them, no matter what form the opposition to them—and him—took.

He was also our source of joy and never failed to spread happiness, regardless of the company he was in. I admired his capacity to bridge social gaps with tremendous ease—he was as comfortable having *lassi* in the interiors of Rajasthan as he was at a sit-down dinner in the company of diplomats and industrialists in Geneva. He was able to strike a chord with his listeners—be it the fishermen of coastal Andhra Pradesh or a fresh batch of IAS officers. He spoke from his heart and was able to instantly connect with people. We have a lot to live up to, and I am sure we will be able to make him proud of us, just as we are proud of him. We feel him around us, watching over us with a smile, up there, somewhere . . . .

Sachin

(Sachin)

Early Years

Strength does not come from physical capacity. It comes from an indomitable will.

—M.K. Gandhi

- Son of Jai Dayal Singh and Baldeyi
- Born: The day after Diwali, 1945
- Village: Baidpura, Ghaziabad, Uttar Pradesh
- Finished school: April 1963
- Joined Air Force: June 1964
- Married: March 12, 1974

❋ *Even after shifting to Delhi, Pilot kept close connections with his family in the village. Here he is seen with his mother (sitting, front row), his sister and his nephews.*

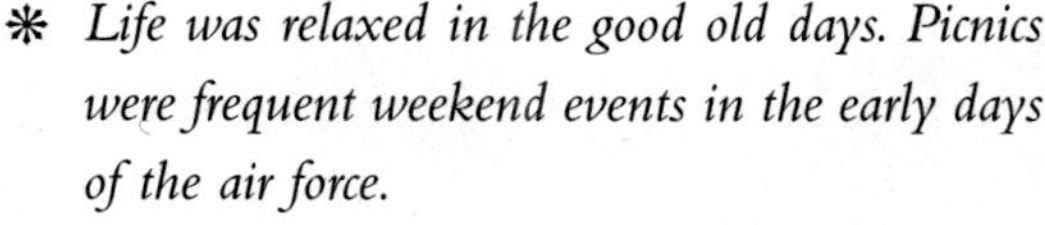

❋ *Life was relaxed in the good old days. Picnics were frequent weekend events in the early days of the air force.*

❋ *Regular evenings with brother officers at the Air Force mess in Guwahati.*

Running barefoot in the fields, raiding the sugarcane crop, stealing mangoes from orchards, swimming in the village ponds with the cows—these were familiar scenes from Rajesh Pilot's early years. The first ten years of his life were typical of that of a village boy—carefree, fun-filled and simple. At the age of 11 tragedy struck the family. His father, the breadwinner of the family, passed away. He had to take care of a mother, two sisters of marriageable age and the education of a younger brother. Most important he had to grow up in a hurry in order to shoulder all these responsibilities. Rajesh moved to Delhi to work in his cousin's dairy to support the family. His early years were pure hard work. He woke up at the crack of dawn, milked the cows, distributed the milk in the Lutyen bungalows in Delhi and then, rushed to school. Upon his return he milked the cows again, distributed the milk, cleaned the dairy and then attacked his textbooks under the lamp-post.

People remember him as a man of integrity and confidence. But few knew him as a boy who, upon being singled out in the school assembly for wearing a torn uniform, had the strength to point out that though torn and old, it was clean. This prompted the principal to enlist him in the NCC so he would get a free uniform. There were times when he sold newspapers at traffic lights. But through all this, the young boy grew up believing that poverty was not a stigma. He imbibed constantly from life and taught himself to be honest and courageous. He managed to get his two sisters married and educate his younger brother who, unfortunately, passed away at the age of 18. He grew up into a young man who believed that no condition was permanent and one could rise out of poverty by hard work. It was his hard work and beliefs that saw him rise from a *doodhwala* to a highly popular leader.

❋ Rajesh Pilot with his mother (left) and older sister.

* ***Left, above & below:*** *March 12, 1974. Another milestone: His marriage to Rama was completely arranged. The ceremonies were simple and typically 'Gujjar'.*

* *Just after the* pheras *Pilot shares a cup of tea with his father-in-law, Choudhary Nain Singh (extreme left) and his cousin Nathi Singh, whose dairy he had worked in as a boy.*

✻ *Early days of marriage with Gyan Chand, an old friend of his.*

Air Force Days

- OCTOBER 29, 1966: Commissioned as Pilot Officer
- FIRST POSTING : Guwahati
- SECOND POSTING: Kalaikunda
- THIRD POSTING: Sarsawa, Saharanpur
- LAST POSTING: New Delhi

❋ *Dad spent close to six years in the north-eastern sector and loved every minute of it. He maintained his relationships with all his friends of those days till the very end. Whenever they were together, they reminisced about their 'good old days'. His air force friends remained his closest buddies.*

Pilot Officer Rajeshwar Prasad and his two mates pooled in money and bought an imported car—a Morris Minor. The whole gang would get ready in the evenings and go for a round of the town in that car. Then one day one of them lent the car to a friend of his who used it to haul cement and the car was written off! It was no big deal. It was just a car. That was the attitude in those days. That was the depth of friendship when Pilot was in the air force. They lived for that day and believed in two words very strongly—No Problem. Everything and anything was No Problem. This was a time in Pilot Officer Rajeshwar Prasad's life when he emerged from the shadows.

Right through his schooldays he was an observer but in the air force he found his feet and his personality blossomed. He made very close and good friends who continue to support and love his family evenafter he has gone. That was probably the only time when his responsibilities were fewer and he enjoyed some carefree bachelor days. He saw action in 1971 during the war with Pakistan. He never knew which sortie would be the last one. But his spirits were high and he was anxious to defend the country. He won a medal for bravery after the war.

Known as Prasad, Dad was a friendly guy who got along with everyone and was known for his happy-go-lucky nature. Typical of the armed forces' ethos, there were some married families in the station whose houses were raided by the bachelors at night. Sleepy wives good naturedly made egg and toast for all of them. In this phase of life Rajesh learnt to share and care: this was probably the first semblance of family life that he witnessed. He grew and matured as a person. He met and worked with many different people in his various postings, learning to respect human nature and accommodate individual idiosyncrasies.

Once while waiting for a VIP to land at their base, he told his friends that one day they would all be standing there to receive him. 'I will be the VIP.' A round of laughter followed and somebody said, '*Doodhiya*, that will be the day . . . '. Little did they realise how prophetic Rajesh Pilot's words were to be.

* *At a briefing at an operational base somewhere in the north-east sector. The zest, patriotism and commitment to his country brought out the best in him. Nothing was too difficult—it simply had to be done!*

* *On winter mornings a member of the team would wake up on time, look out of the window and decide whether there was enough visibility for flying. On cloudy and foggy days, when there was no flying, everyone slept late. Life's simple pleasures, stolen moments of hostel-like capers—helped to keep a smile on faces who had a brush with death almost every day.*

* ***Page 28:*** *It is every fighter pilot's dream to fly the F-16. Rajesh Pilot's chance came as a minister, while he was on an official trip to the Netherlands.*

Page 29: *Ready to take off—in the cockpit of an F-16 at a Nato base in Europe.*

PLAYER

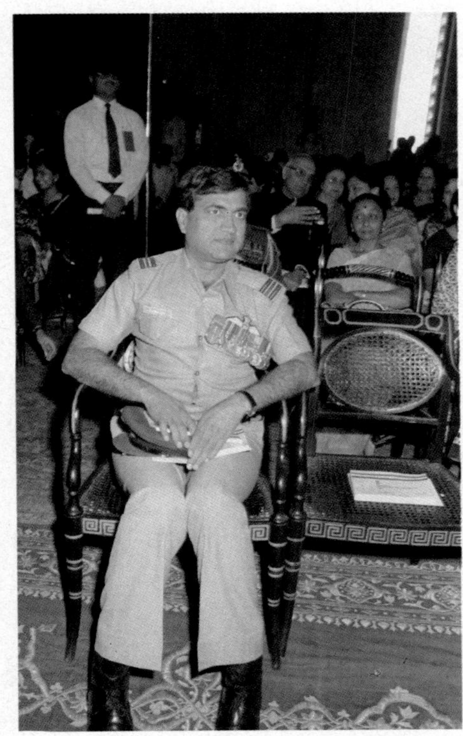

* *Even though a minister at the Centre, Rajesh Pilot loved getting back into his uniform—though relegated then only for ceremonial purposes.*

Above: *On Air Force Day, he is flanked by the Chief of Air Staff, S.K. Kaul (right) and Air Chief Marshal N.C. Suri (retd.).*

Right: *Seated in Rashtrapati Bhavan's glittering Ashoka hall to witness an award being presented to a former air force colleague.*

Facing page: *Flying was a passion with Rajesh Pilot—he flew whenever he got a chance even after leaving the air force.*

The Shaping of a Politician

When a man works for an ideal, he becomes irresistible.

—M.K. Gandhi

- 1980: Elected Member of Parliament from Bharatpur
- 1984: Elected from Dausa
- 1989: Lost from Bharatpur
- 1991: Elected from Dausa
- 1996: Elected from Dausa
- 1998: Elected from Dausa
- 1999: Elected from Dausa

✻ 'As you sow, so shall you reap. *In 1981, planting a sapling in his constituency.*

'Simple living and high thinking' was Pilot's motto in life. In 1979 when Rajesh Pilot (then Rajeshwar Prasad) walked into the AICC office to collect his symbol for the election, he asked the Congressman in charge to point out Bharatpur on the map of India, for he had not heard of it. People said: What is wrong with Mrs Gandhi? She gives tickets to just anybody. When he went to file his nomination papers in Bharatpur, people told him they only knew that a pilot was coming to contest the elections. He said: 'You can call me a donkey, but make me win the election.' It was on that day that Rajeshwar Prasad became Rajesh Pilot. The name changed his destiny. He had opted for politics to find a forum to help the underprivileged and farmers. He understood their plight and their demands. His aim was to become their mouthpiece. He was young, he was passionate, he was honest and he had dreams—dreams that had to be realised. He wanted to help the people of his constituency, of his India. He felt he was one of the underprivileged who had made it somewhere in society, so he considered it his duty to help others like himself.

❋ *A hero's welcome: Rajesh Pilot always enjoyed the love of the people wherever he went. His easy-going nature won him the loyalty of friends and acquaintances.*

From the day he became an MP his house was open to anyone from any part of the country who could come and stay there, whether it was to visit a sick relative or take an entrance exam. He brought into day-to-day life a quality of sharing and caring for other human beings. He toured his constituency and got to know everyone. His rural background was an asset. People felt connected to him. They felt understood by him. His easy-going, humble, informal nature made him popular and their true representative. He talked about his early days and encouraged people to try to achieve big things in life and improve their conditions. He enjoyed simple food and while on tour, always ate in some village. His patience and tolerant nature made it easy for people to approach him. He was probably the only MP who practised democracy to the level that people in his constituency came and fought with him, considering it their right to do so. He was the first to admit a mistake. Whatever he gave to the people, was returned to him tenfold with God's grace.

* *His early speeches were short and direct. Slowly he matured into a powerful orator and a seasoned politician.*

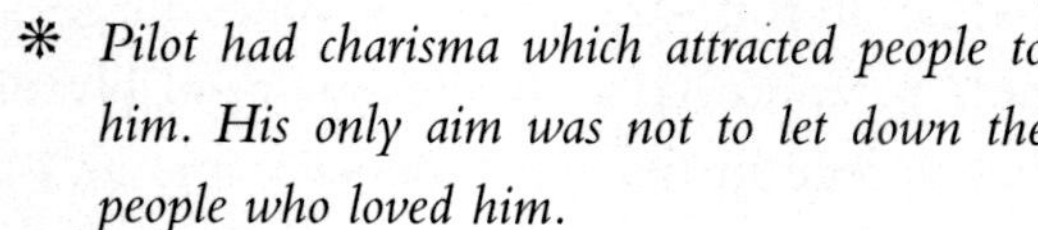

* *Pilot had charisma which attracted people to him. His only aim was not to let down the people who loved him.*

* *An unpretentious man who attended any function, large or small, he is seen here in a small meeting in a* tehsil *in his constituency.*

* *'You can achieve anything you want, if you set your mind to it.' This was the message of Rajesh Pilot's autobiographical book,* Flight to Parliament, *released by Lok Sabha Speaker Balram Jakhar in 1982.*

* *A warm welcome—his popularity increased with time. His weekend visits to his constituency, which remained a regular feature, went a long way in helping him to keep a finger on the pulse of his people's concerns and problems. No wonder then, that he was known as 'the man of the masses'.*

✻ *At a public meeting in Bharatpur with his wife Rama. Attending numerous functions and meetings with her husband, Rama's presence and interest was reassuring to the women who saw in her, hope for their upliftment.*

* *Dad was worth his weight in gold! But here, he is being weighed in coins at Dausa. An old tradition in the state, money thus collected was diverted for welfare activities.*

Facing page: *During one of the* Jansampark *in Dausa.*

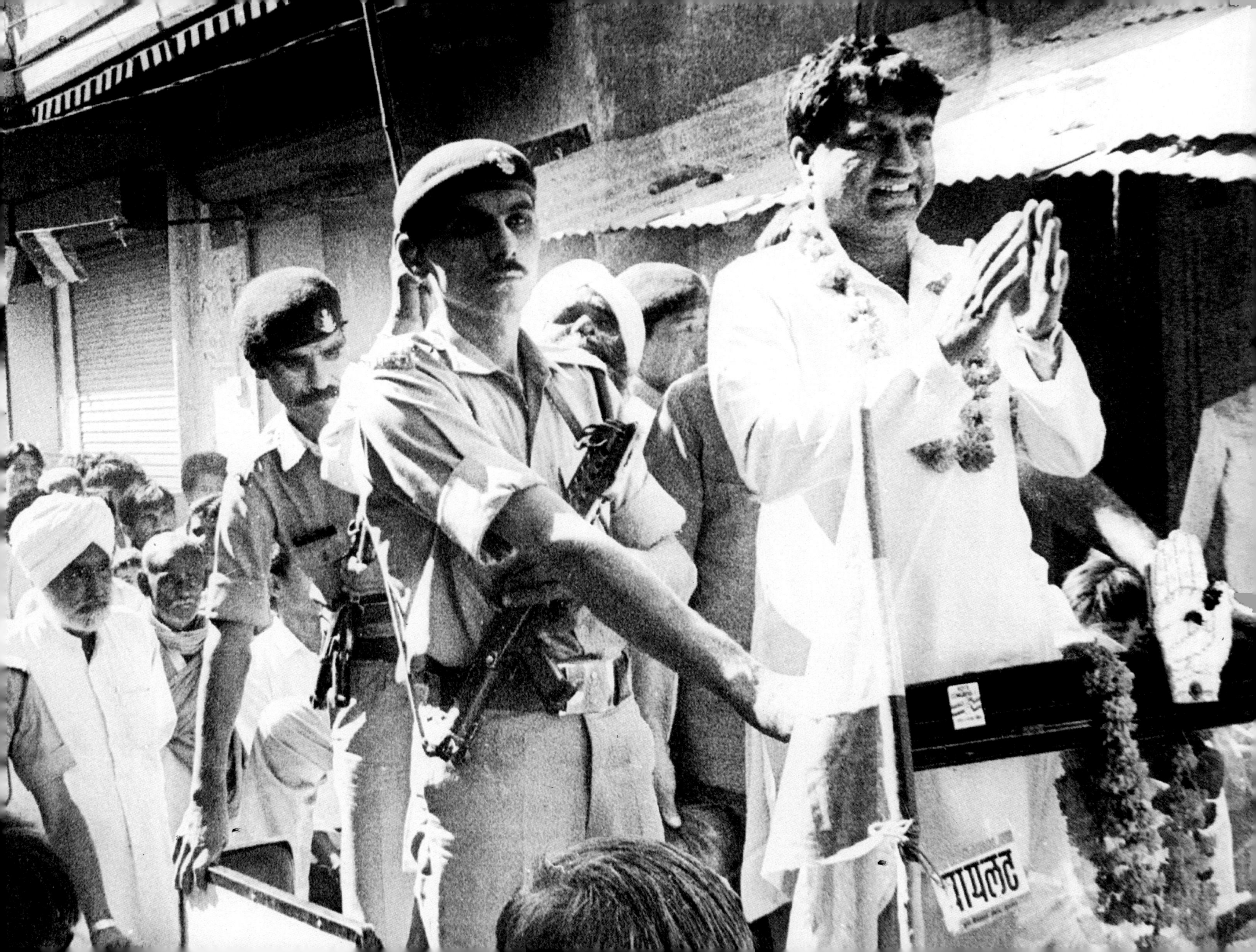

✻ *Mrs Indira Gandhi looked on him as a bright, young, honest and uninhibited young man familiar with the north-east. She sent him as an observer for elections in Nagaland.*

Pilot first met Mrs Gandhi in 1979 to request her for an election ticket. She advised him to continue with the air force as he had young children to bring up and politics was not a very stable profession. He calmly told her that he had come for her blessings, not her advice. This really impressed her and she gave him a ticket just a month later.

** Rajiv Gandhi and he shared a passion for flying and a similar dream for India. As a result it was during Rajiv Gandhi's tenure as Prime Minister that two very important Accords, those of Kashmir and Assam were signed.*

✻ *Receiving President Sanjiva Reddy in his constituency—Bharatpur.*

Facing page: *At a* kisan *rally in Samalkha, Haryana, where he founded the* Jai Jawan Jai Kisan Trust. *From top left clockwise are: Darbara Singh, Chief Minister of Punjab; Rama Pilot; Rajesh Pilot; Vir Bhadra Singh, Chief Minister of Himachal Pradesh; Bhagwat Jha Azad, Chief Minister of Bihar and Farooq Abdullah, Chief Minister of Jammu & Kashmir.*

❋ *President Giani Zail Singh found in Pilot, an ambitious man from a similar rural background like himself.*

⁕ *President K.R. Narayanan, then the Vice-President, releasing a departmental book.*

✻ *Dad was very fond of Kashmir and its people. Here he is with Prime Minister Rajiv Gandhi (centre) and the Jammu & Kashmir Chief Minister Farooq Abdullah in the PM's aircraft on their way to Srinagar for the Kashmir Accord.*

* *He spent as many as six years in the north-east as a pilot officer which gave him a deep insight into the problems of that sector. Here he is seen signing the Assam Accord with the Chief Minister Hiteshwar Saikia.*

✻ *As Minister for Communications, on a brief visit to Geneva to attend a conference.*

✻ *As the Minister for Surface Transport he met his counterpart in the Netherlands in 1988.*

Facing page: *Old habits die hard. Map reading for reference—a habit carried forward from his air force days.*

ARCTIC OCEAN
ATLANTIC OCEAN
PACIFIC OCEAN
INDIAN OCEAN
WORLD
POLITICAL
CHINA
AFGHANISTAN
PAKISTAN
INDIA
RAILWAYS
TIBET
BURMA
ARABIAN SEA
BAY OF BENGAL
INDIAN OCEAN
RAJASTHAN
ROAD GUIDE & POLITICAL
PAKISTAN
1981

✻ *Rajesh Pilot's spontaneity won him many hearts. As Minister for Surface Transport, he surprised everyone on a visit to Visakhapatnam Port in 1986 when he jumped on to a parapet to address the union workers.*

Inspecting the Guard of Honour. Dad respected the uniform because it had been a part of him for many years. Even when he became the Inspector *from the* Inspected, *his respect for the uniform only grew.*

Facing page: *A moment of great joy—unfurling the national flag, surrounded by people whose hopes and aspirations it represented.*

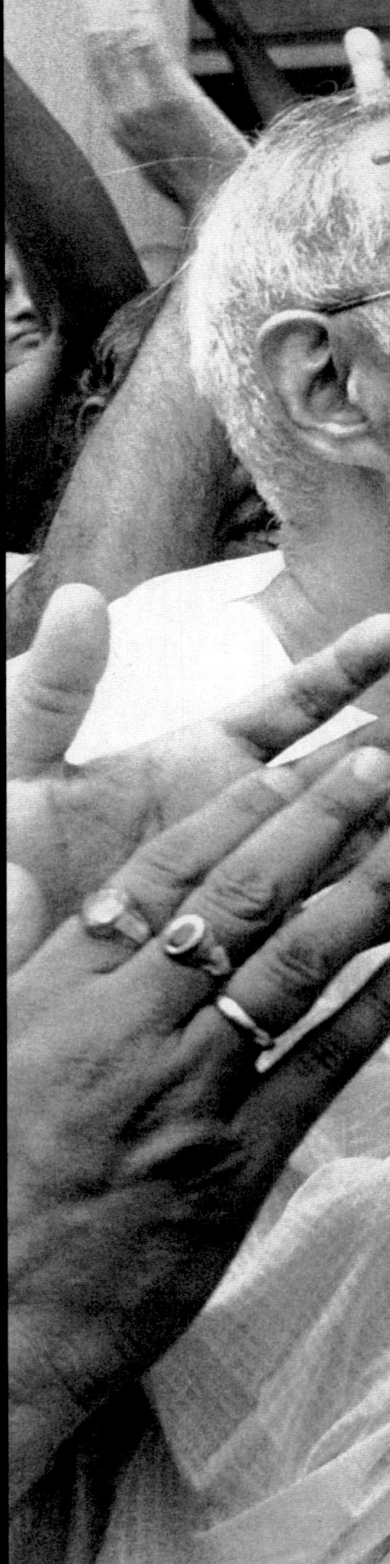

✻ ***Left:*** *For every occasion—Diwali, Holi, Christmas and birthdays—Dad would arrange* Bada Khaana *for the security guards at home.*

Below: *He loved drinking tea out of a* kulhar, *preferring it over more fancy cups and mugs.*

✻ ***Facing page:*** *Sharing a* hookah *with a delegation who had come home. Sharing or offering the* hookah *is a mark of respect or honour to a guest in the villages.*

* *Pilot's tours in the constituency entailed at least 8-10 arranged meetings but there were frequent halts where he just stopped the jeep and people gathered under a tree to discuss their problems.*

❋ *He met many interesting people on his travels. Here he is in Jaisalmer with Karna Bheel, the man who went into the* Guinness Book of World Records *for having the longest moustache in the world.*

❋ The Jammu, Kashmir and Ladakh sector was an area where Pilot really concentrated. He visited that area at the height of militancy and won many hearts. People there found someone to trust and believe in. It was during these trips that there were many assassination attempts on his life. But he still persisted in going there and always fought for their cause with the union government.

❊ *Holding court: It was always Open House at the Pilot house in New Delhi. Other than meeting people in the mornings, Rajesh Pilot would always find the time, no matter what time of day, to listen to their woes and promise succour. Words like parochialism did not exist in his dictionary.*

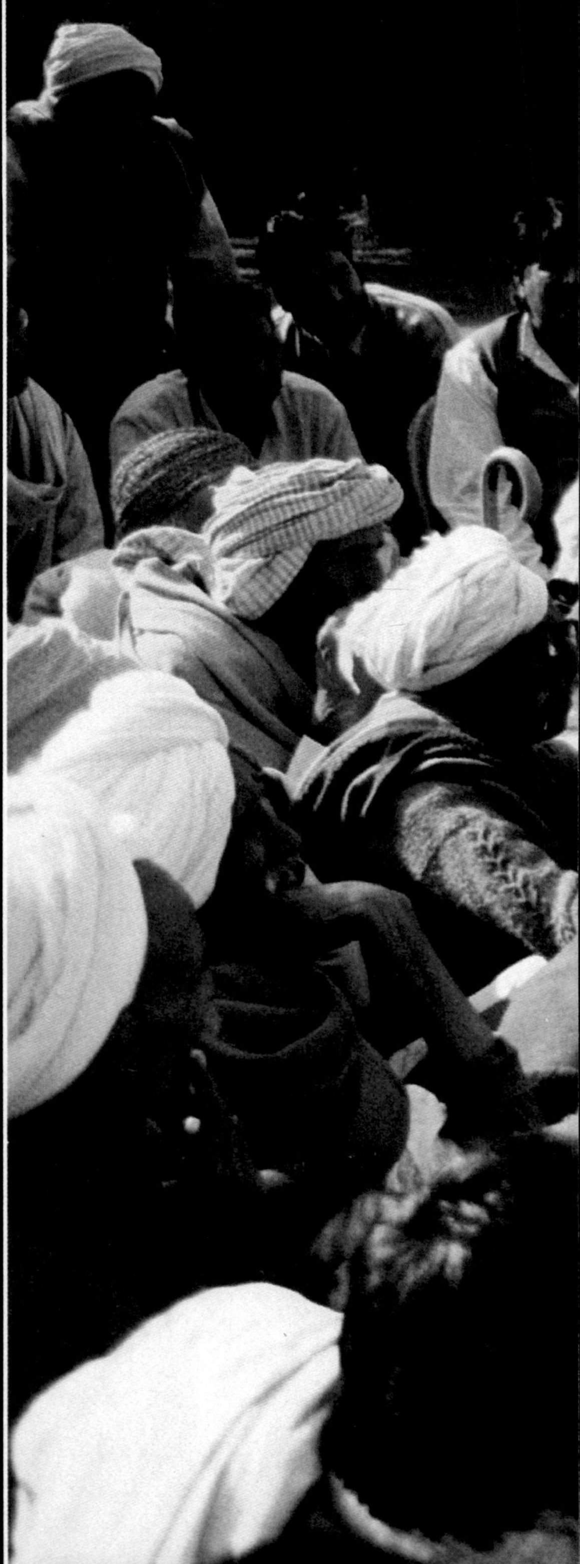

A National Leader Emerges

Manliness consists not in bluff, bravado or lordliness. It consists in daring to do the right and facing consequences, whether it is in matters social, political or other. It consists in deeds, not in words.

— M.K. Gandhi

Dhir

- 1985: Minister for Surface Transport
- 1991: Minister for Communications
- 1993: Minister for Internal Security
- 1995: Minister for Environment

✻ *Pilot was very popular in the southern part of the country and visited it often. On this trip he was given a grand welcome and greeted with an enormous* maala *which is very popular in south India.*

Little did the boy who sold milk on Akbar Road realise, that one day he would be living in the very same house. 'God has been very kind', were words he repeated nearly every day. He did not forget his roots and never took his success for granted. Hence each day was an opportunity for him to serve his country.

He had strong views on democracy, honesty and truth. They were his convictions and he stuck to them through bad and good times. His rise to national politics was very swift. At a relatively young age he had made a base in the country. He was popular with the masses. Again, his humble background while being a source of encouragement to the weaker section of society, helped him bridge the usual gap between the people and a political leader. He travelled extensively during these years. He was a man who was liked and appreciated and most important, respected even by opposition members. He had a knack for establishing a rapport with people.

As a Minister he was very conscientious. He concentrated on his department. While he was the Surface Transport Minister he would just board the city transport buses to check the services. As Communications Minister he made sure that every village had an STD/ISD telephone. He ensured free telephones at airports and in the Emergency Room of hospitals. His dream was to bridge the immense gap between the villages in India and the cities. He wanted the villages to be modern and have modern amenities. He felt that India could only be strong and a world power once the villages had been modernised and poverty had been eradicated. He encouraged the setting up of industries in villages because that would give employment to the people. The few times that he went abroad he would study the methods and technology used there and see how he could adapt them to India.

An area which was dear to him was Jammu & Kashmir and the north-east which he visited often as Internal Security Minister. He believed that Kashmir was an integral part of India and visited there often to reassure the people that there was someone in the centre looking out for their interests.

He also started a trust called *Jai Jawan Jai Kisan Trust* which provided pension to old people and widows, financed education and schools and hospitals. The Trust carries on with Rajesh Pilot's work even now, ensuring that the dreams, the visions he had for India live on . . . .

❋ *At a* bhumi pujan *for a school in Amber.*

✻ ***Facing page:*** *As Minister for Surface Transport, meeting the crew on a ship.*

Taking the salute for a Guard of Honour.

✻ *He preferred travelling by air because he was always in a hurry and had too much to do. It was a standard joke in political circles that Pilot had just 'left' the air force, not his penchant for aircraft.*

✻ *In his years as Minister for Surface Transport, whenever Pilot visited a port, he made it a point to meet all the workers. He knew that they were the cornerstone of the industry and did not always get enough recognition. In his own way he tried to give them as much recognition and support as he could.*

❋ Cochin Shipyard, 1986. Pilot was a man who was not merely satisfied with the result—he had a healthy curiosity in how the relevant apparatus worked.

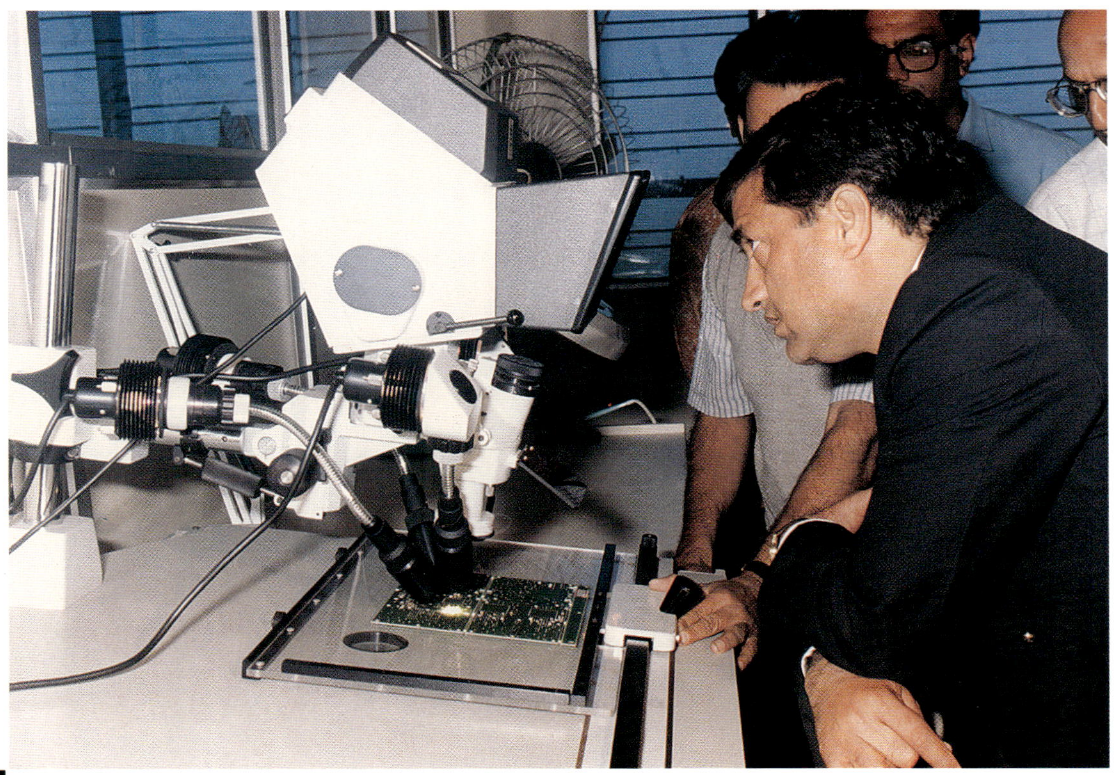

❋ Pilot was very proud of India's cultural heritage. His respect for Indian tradition was well known.

❋ *Usually while driving back from the constituency he would stop the convoy to eat at one of the* dhabas*, his favourite being* makki ki roti *and* sarson ka saag. *He was always concerned about the people with him— security guards and workers, and shared his food with them, bought them fruit or tea and made them feel looked after.*

N. D. TEWARI
CHAIRMAN

⁂ *Pilot was a fitness freak. He exercised daily, wherever he was. He believed that a healthy body made one more alert. Any physical activity was more than welcome.*

***Right:** Self-loading a rifle and carbine during a visit to the training centre of the Special Security Forces in Hyderabad in 1994.*

***Facing page:** Rajesh Pilot shares a joke and a telephonic conversation, with a senior colleague in the ministry, N.D. Tiwari. His attendance here marked a new phase in connecting people—through the Haldwani electronic exchange, 1992.*

* *Turban firmly in place, Rajesh Pilot addresses a gathering of the* Akhil Bhartiya Majdoor Maha Panchayat *at New Delhi's Ramlila grounds in 1994. Says daughter Sarika, 'He derived his strength not from his position or power, but from the faith and love of the people.'*

Facing page: *Conditions in the country made it necessary for Rajesh Pilot to carry a security cordon with him—such as when campaigning for the Lok Sabha elections in 1996.*

Vote for

❋ *His smile was his trademark and his biggest legacy. He encouraged everyone to smile through their lives in good times and bad times.*

❋ ***Facing page:*** *On his election campaign for president of the Congress Parliamentary Party against Sitaram Kesri in 1998, Pilot is fêted by Salman Khurshid (left) and Oscar Fernandes (right).*

Last words. It was moments after addressing an audience from this podium in Dausa on June 11, 2000, that Rajesh Pilot in the driver's seat of a jeep, collided with a truck, abruptly cutting short a brilliant political career.

Tributes

A career of great promise and significance has been cut short in its prime. Mr Pilot was a staunch nationalist who identified himself with the aspirations of the people, especially deprived sections of our society. His absence will be keenly felt in Parliament and in the nation as a whole. I extend my heartfelt condolences to his bereaved wife, the members of his family and a large number of his associates.

President K.R. Narayanan

We had lot of expectations from him. The country also needed a leader like him. Whether in power or in opposition, the fighter leader served the nation.

Prime Minister Atal Behari Vajpayee

A renowned social and political worker, Shri Pilot was an effective administrator and an able parliamentarian. He lost no opportunity to focus the attention of the House to the problems faced by the peasants, ex-servicemen and the deprived sections of the society. Even as an Opposition leader, he maintained decorum while being critical. He was a leader of the masses, a person who would always speak his mind without fear or favour. Shri Rajesh Pilot's impeccable integrity is worthy of emulation.

An instance in 1999 comes to my mind which also highlights Shri Pilot's exemplary sense of integrity. During the Twelfth Lok Sabha, on 8th March, 1999, immediately after Question Hour, there was a demand from some Members in the House for a statement by a Minister, who had resigned from the Union Council of Ministers. Shri Pilot also pressed for the statement on the assumption that the item was included in some previous day's List of Business. Later, when it was brought to his notice that the item was not listed, he withdrew his remarks on the floor of the House and as a self-corrective measure, he decided to forego his allowance and sent them a cheque of Rs 500 for being deposited in the Lok Sabha Secretariat Employees' Welfare Fund.

Lok Sabha Speaker G.M.C. Balayogi

Not only the Congress Party, but his followers, his admirers throughout the country and this House which he represented for six terms, have lost a most dynamic and dedicated leader. His deep concern for the poor, for the farmers, for the labourers, for the backward classes in general, his frank and candid demeanour earned him a very special place in the hearts of the people of our country. On Shri Rajesh Pilot's passing away we mourn the loss of a leader of great capability and promise. We shall all miss him greatly. He is no longer amongst us. But his memory and his work will endure.

Congress President Sonia Gandhi

A Family United

Love never claims; it ever gives. Love ever suffers, never resents, never revenges itself.

—M.K. Gandhi

- March 12, 1974: Married to Rama
- April 17, 1975: Daughter Sarika was born
- September 7, 1977: Son Sachin was born
- February 6, 2000: Daughter married Vishal Chaudhry

❋ *Rajesh Pilot loved relaxing in his garden, and the lawn behind the house was where he spent quiet moments with the family. Never ostentatious in his life, even his garden furniture consisted of simple bulrush stalk chairs,* moodhas *and* charpoys.

'Never do anything you cannot tell the world,' Pilot often told his family. He felt that life should be an open book which anyone could look into at any time . . . . That, he thought, made individuals responsible for their actions. He and Rama brought up the children in a typical middle class style. They studied at the Air Force school and later he gave them his full support to choose their careers. He was a democratic man even with his family, believing that every member of the family had a right to have an opinion and influence any decision.

In 1974 when he got married he told his wife he had only Rs 5000 for the honeymoon. For the first two days they stayed in a five-star hotel, the next two days in a three-star and by the end of their honeymoon they were in a hotel that charged Rs 25 per night.

As the family grew he took his responsibility as a father very seriously. Even with increasing demands on his time he always had time for his children. For him family came first and he took his wife and children along on many of his tours.

As the children grew up he encouraged Rama to take an active interest in politics again, guiding and supporting her. As a family they took many holidays together—mostly weekend getaways. These short breaks away from work really rejuvenated him. They also gave the family beautiful memories which are all the more precious now. He was very involved in his children's lives and knew exactly what they were up to. Whatever the time, he always waited up for them to come home at night when they were out with friends.

When the time came for the children to step out of home, he encouraged them to choose the careers that attracted them the most. He stressed the importance of education, so when his son was selected in Wharton School in Philadelphia, he was jubilant. But he missed him sorely and actually called him in the US every day. He loved his family and enjoyed their company the most. The whole family functioned as a unit. Pilot ensured that he shared his values with the family so every one had a similar line of thought on most issues. He firmly believed that the most important gifts one could give one's children were a sound value system and a good education which would enable them to take care of themselves in future. That was his way of securing his children's future. The Pilot family shared 25 years of bliss together—those 25 years are now equal to as many lifetimes of happiness for the family that remains.

* *A simple love story. Pilot was able to find the time for holidays to some of the country's famous tourist spots. A visit to the Taj Mahal with Rama and Sachin.*

* *In the garden of their first official residence in New Delhi at 3, Safdarjung Road.*

❋ *Love means sharing and togetherness.*

Above: *Soul mates at home, Rama stood by her husband, taking a keen interest in his professional activities.*

Right: *The Pilot juniors attempt to emulate their parents —clothes and all!*

THE TIMES OF INDIA

❋ *He once told the children, 'If you can steal one paisa you can steal a million. Don't let your resolve weaken even for a second or you are lost for life. It is that split second decision that can shape you for the rest of your life.'*

✻ *The children were his closest allies and his worst critics. He gave them the position and space in his life to be able to play those roles.*

✻ *Sachin Pilot sports his father's* safa, *which later became his trademark. Having switched to politics, Pilot was often identified by his turban. It also established an immediate bond with people from the countryside and his constituency.*

❋ *Through happiness and tragedy, Rama and Rajesh Pilot were to prove a source of great strength to each other. It was rare to see them without a smile on their faces.*

✻ *Stolen moments together. The Pilot family on the rear lawn of 10, Akbar Road, Rajesh Pilot's last official residence in Delhi. As Sachin and Sarika grew older, instead of growing apart, the family grew together despite their pressing schedules.*

✻ Sachin and Sarika flank their parents on the millennium eve, December 31, 1999.

❋ *Love meant a cosy foursome—in days when the older and younger generations go their own way, the Pilots enjoyed each other's company. 'We were always a close family,' says Sachin, 'but of late the relationship had changed from a tradition parent-child one to that of friendship.' 'Dad,' adds Sarika, 'was our closest friend.'*

❋ *The family had opportunities to travel extensively in India and to a few countries abroad. Pilot maintained that travel was one of the best forms of education. He intended the children to see the difference between the two and imbibe the best from both worlds. The budget was usually tight but the fun was unlimited.*

❋ *Even after the children grew up dinners were a family affair after the parents came back from an evening out.*

Facing page: *Flying high and together—Rama and Rajesh.*

❋ *Rajesh Pilot's sartorial style (here with friends in Shillong) adapted itself to fit different moods and places. Here, he relaxes in short sleeves and a hat, but he could wear a* salwar-kurta *in Jammu and Kashmir with as much panache as he would sport a* lungi *in the South.*

❋ *An Australian family friend shares an early morning with the Pilots on the lawn. Rajesh Pilot always had his tea, and read his newspapers outdoors.*

✻ *Pilot always kept a pet. He loved dogs. He took care of them personally, made sure they were fed and bathed them on weekends. The dogs, in turn, trailed after him wherever he went.*

❋ He was truly a multifaceted man. There were things he enjoyed doing which were so simple like sliding in the snow, playing Holi or playing cricket with the children. His body language (see pics) distinctly conveyed that he was comfortable being himself. On the other hand he gave moving speeches and was a national leader and a constant source of support to thousands of people.

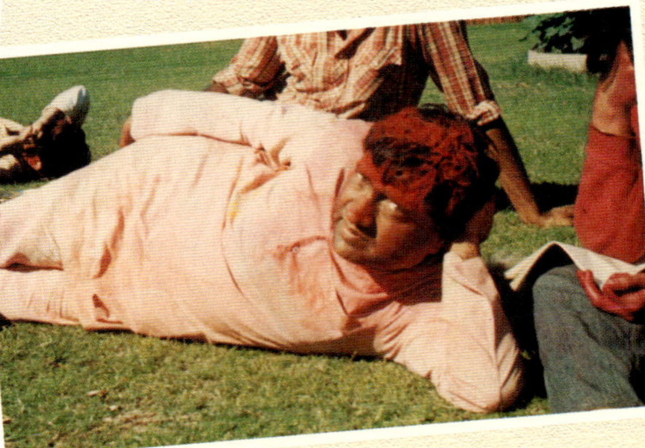

❋ *Sarika's wedding was an emotional affair for him. He kept the wedding simple and very low key. Only close friends and relatives were invited. The wedding took place at 10, Akbar Road, New Delhi.*

Left: *Sarika shares a cup of tea with her father a day before her wedding.*

Below (left & right): *Smiles, goodwill, cheer and excitement.*

Facing page: *On Sarika's* Mehandiraat *just before the wedding.*

❋ ***Right:*** *The family taking Sarika to the mandap.*

Middle: *With son-in-law Vishal.*

Below: *At the* vidayi. *Pilot tried to put on a brave front through the wedding but broke down at the end.*

Facing page: *Resplendent in their traditional red and yellow* safas, *the bride's family waits with garlands to welcome the* baraat.

❋ *Then one day he was gone from our lives just like that. Though no more with us physically, he remains with us in spirit forever.*